D1491603

The Phantom of the Opera

Gaston Leroux
Retold by Kate Knighton

Illustrated by Victor Tavares

Reading consultant: Alison Kelly
Roehampton University

Contents

Chapter 1   The Opera House   3

Chapter 2   A surprising voice   12

Chapter 3   The phantom's demands   20

Chapter 4   The angel of music   25

Chapter 5   An unforgettable performance   34

Chapter 6   Underground secrets   42

Chapter 7   A disappearing act   50

Chapter 8   The phantom's lair   56

This book is set in Paris, France and some of the characters use French words. Mademoiselle (say mad-mwa-zel) means Miss and Monsieur (say muhss-yuh) means Sir.

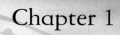

Chapter 1

The Opera House

The Phantom of the Opera isn't just another ghost story. The phantom really existed, secretly roaming the grand halls of the Paris Opera House...

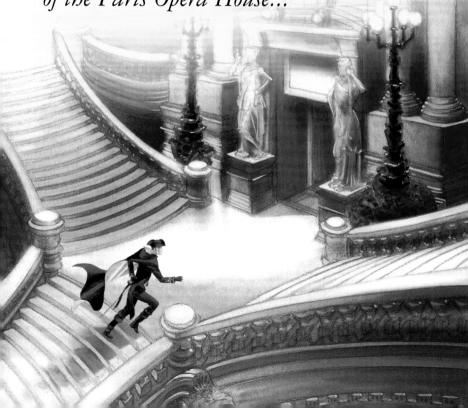

The air in the opera house was humming with excitement. It was the first night under new management. Voices were warming up with high trills...

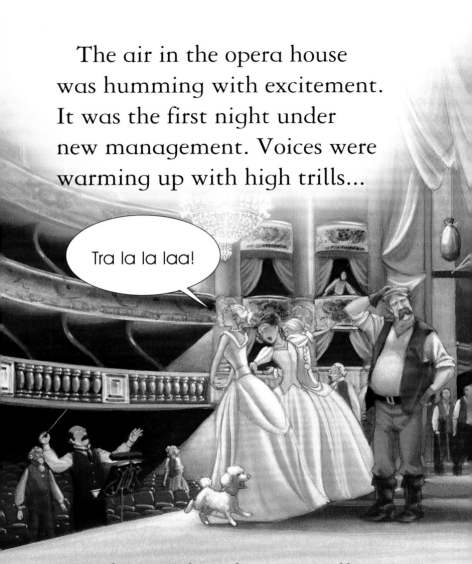

...and stage-hands were milling around, looking for props.

The star of the show,
Carlotta, stomped around,
complaining.

I said
RED grapes
you fool!

"How can I be expected to sing,"
she wailed, to no one in particular,
"when my throat hurts from all
the smoke in this horrible city?"

Down the corridor from Carlotta, dancers fussed and fiddled with their costumes.

But in one dressing room the evening's performance was the last thing anyone was thinking about...

"I heard the ghost has different heads that he changes as he pleases," said one of the dancers.

"I've heard he has no nose!" cried another, whose own nose was widely admired.

"You're all wrong," said a third dancer, smugly. "I've seen the phantom with my very own eyes." The others turned to stare at her.

"He has *one* head and you could mistake him for a gentleman in his long black cloak and fine hat. But I don't know about his nose, because his face was covered with a mask."

"A mask?" the girls cried.

The dancer paused dramatically. "They say the phantom's face is SO horrific and SO frightening, it would make a grown man weep!"

"Arrgh!" screamed the girls.

"Enough of that nonsense!" interrupted Madame G, who was in charge of the show. "We have a crisis. Carlotta is refusing to sing."

The girls began to whisper among themselves.

Go on!

They dragged a shy girl named Christine over to Madame G. "Christine can do it!"

"But she doesn't know the part!" cried Madame.

"I do," said Christine softly, "I sing it every night after the show." Madame looked her up and down and sighed. "What choice do I have? Well, get into costume. Go!"

Chapter 2

A surprising voice

The audience waited eagerly in their red velvet seats. They gazed up at the huge glass chandelier, suspended from the painted ceiling. Slowly, the lights dimmed...

The curtains went up and the cast swarmed onto the vast stage. Their voices filled the air like a chorus of angels and their bright costumes glittered as they danced.

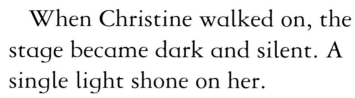

When Christine walked on, the stage became dark and silent. A single light shone on her.

She opened her mouth and sang from her heart. It was the sweetest, most beautiful sound.

When she finished, there was silence for a moment, before loud applause erupted. The noise rang dizzily in Christine's ears and she fainted.

The audience watched in silence, as Christine's limp body was picked up and carried offstage.

She was placed in a chair in her dressing room. Madame G thrust smelling salts under her nose and she blinked open her eyes.

"My dear, you were magnificent!" said Madame G, fanning her with a handkerchief. "And you have a visitor. He's a Count!" she whispered excitedly, before rushing out.

A handsome young man came into the room. "Mademoiselle," he said, tipping his hat.

"Count, do excuse me," Christine said, trying to stand up.

"No, please rest," said the Count. "You had quite a turn."

"I just came to say," he went on, "I'm a huge fan of the opera and I thought you were wonderful. You should sing every night!"

Christine blushed. "I was just standing in for Carlotta."

"You're a million times better than her," he declared. "Anyway, I'd better go. Good night."

The Count shut the door behind him and leaned against it for a moment. He could hear a deep, male voice coming from the room.

"But there was no one else in there..." he mumbled.

He had his ear to the door when a couple of dancers came by, so he quickly walked away.

Chapter 3

The phantom's demands

"What is the meaning of this?"
The new manager of the opera
house waved a piece of paper at
Madame G.

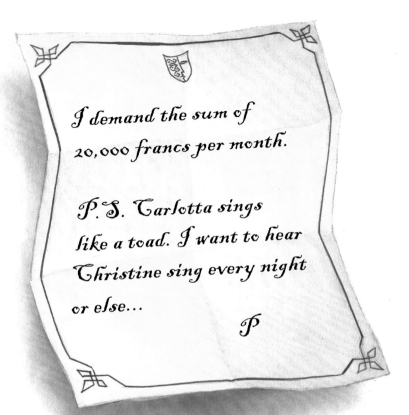

I demand the sum of
20,000 francs per month.

P.S. Carlotta sings
like a toad. I want to hear
Christine sing every night
or else...

P

"It's the phantom," she said
nervously. "I tell the girls he isn't
real. But the truth is, I've worked
here for twenty years and we
have always given in to him." She
shuddered. "If we don't, he'll make
big trouble."

21

"Phantom? You mean a ghost?" said the manager. "Hah! If some crook who skulks around *my* opera house thinks he can swindle money out of *me*, he's got another think coming!"

Suddenly, the door swung open and a stagehand burst in. "It's Pico! He's been taken!"

Pico was the manager's beloved pet dog.

"My little Pico! What? How?" spluttered the manager.

"I heard Pico barking and saw a man in a cloak in the shadows!"

Madame G shivered. "It's the phantom. Mark my words, manager. Pay up quickly or something dreadful will happen."

Chapter 4

The angel of music

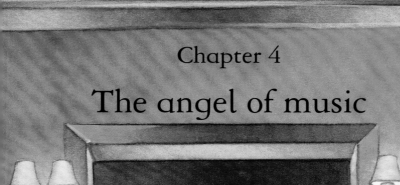

The Count was hovering by
Christine's dressing room. He had
heard about the phantom and was
worried about her, especially after
hearing the strange voice in her
room the week before.

"Count!" Christine almost walked into him as she came out. She looked around nervously and blocked his view into her room.

"Can I help you?" she asked, with a bright smile.

"I just wanted to make sure you were alright after fainting last week..." He paused as he heard the same deep voice coming from her room. "Who's that?"

"Oh, no one," Christine trilled. "I'm fine, thank you, but I must dash..." and she shut the door in his face.

The Count was more puzzled than ever. So he hid behind some costumes and decided to wait.

After a few minutes, Christine came out dressed in a hooded cloak. She rushed down the corridor and out of the opera house.

The Count followed her along
dark, lamplit streets, until they
reached a small, gloomy graveyard.
The moonlight cast creepy shadows
on the ancient stone graves.

The Count watched as Christine knelt by a grave. The church bells began to chime midnight. Sad violin music floated on the air. Christine swayed and sang along to the music as if in a trance. The Count was captivated...

...until he felt a hand on his shoulder that chilled him to the bone.

He looked into a pair of blood-red eyes and let out a scream. "Arrrrgh! The eyes, so red..." the Count spluttered.

As he spoke, the figure vanished. "Count? What eyes? What are you talking about?" asked Christine, running over to him.

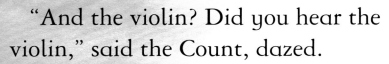

"And the violin? Did you hear the violin," said the Count, dazed.

Christine looked afraid. "Yes, I did," she admitted, "but I don't know who's playing. I come here to sing at my father's grave. Before he died, he told me an angel of music would visit me."

"And has one?" The Count opened his eyes wide.

Yes!

"He comes to the opera house," she said. "He taught me everything I know about singing – but I've never seen him."

"So the voice I heard..."

"Yes, that was him. He says I'll be the most famous singer in Paris! Will you keep it a secret?"

The Count looked serious. "If you want me to," he said. "Now let me walk you back. It's late."

Chapter 5

An unforgettable performance

The next morning was bright and sunny. Carlotta was lying in bed, eating chocolate truffles, when her maid came in with a letter.

"What's this?" Carlotta demanded, her mouth full of chocolate.

If you appear on stage tonight, you must be prepared for a misfortune worse than death!

P

"It's a threat! Someone is telling *me* not to sing. How dare they? Get my things, I'm going straight to the manager."

In less than an hour, Carlotta was in the manager's office. "Monsieur!" she shrieked as she slapped down the letter.

He read it quickly and went pale. "It's the phantom," he muttered.

"Phantom?" Carlotta's ears pricked up. "I'm not afraid of a ghost. I *will* sing tonight!"

That night, the whole cast felt
uneasy. But Carlotta wasn't in the
least worried.

"Phantom? Pah!" she declared.
She fluffed up her costume and
marched on stage.

Carlotta lifted up her arms and opened her mouth wide, but all that came out was a loud, harsh...

The audience gasped. Carlotta continued to croak like a toad and the audience began to laugh.

The manager, who was looking on in disbelief, heard a chilling voice in his ear.

"Carlotta sings tonight to bring the house down..."

"I beg your pardon?" The manager spun around, but the figure behind him had gone.

At that moment, a deafening crack shook the hall. Everyone looked up. The glass chandelier, which sparkled above the audience, was coming loose. Plaster fell from the ceiling in great chunks and the huge light swung dangerously.

The audience began to scream and run from their seats. The singers on stage watched, horrified. With an almighty crash, the chandelier fell, narrowly missing Carlotta.

Then all of the lights went out and a terrifying, ghoulish laugh echoed around the opera house.

Chapter 6

Underground secrets

Backstage, Christine stared at
the madness in terror. As she
watched, a black cloak whirled
around her and she was swept away.

She tried to scream for help,
but her cries were muffled
beneath the cloak.
Blindly, she stumbled
down a flight of stairs
and along a maze of
twisty paths. The
air around her
became colder
and damper as
she struggled
to get free.

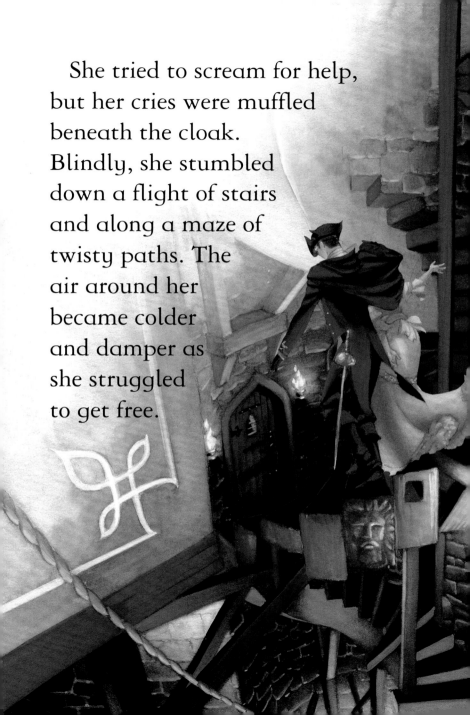

Finally, her captor released his grip. She opened her eyes and blinked. Underneath the opera house was another world.

She saw a misty lake, with stony tunnels leading off in different directions. Huge candles flickered and wax dripped down the dark, dank walls.

"Don't be afraid, Christine," said a deep, melodic voice.

"You!" Christine gasped, spinning around. "My angel of music!"

But he wasn't what she had imagined. She came face to face with a man in a mask...

It was the Phantom of the Opera.

She took a step back, afraid.

"Don't be scared," he said. "I'm your friend. Please trust me!"

He took her shaking hand and led her onto a boat, which sat on the mysterious lake. The boat began to float away. Christine couldn't help but be enchanted.

It's incredible...

"I am the voice you hear. But I'm no angel." He turned his masked face towards the shadows.

"You are! You've been so kind to me." She paused. "Why do you hide down here?"

"It's safe. No one can laugh at my face," the Phantom said sadly.

"It can't be that bad. Will you show me?" Christine asked gently.

"No!" shouted the phantom, suddenly angry. "Of all people I don't want to show you!"

"But you're my friend. I wouldn't turn my back on you," she insisted.

"No Christine!" he said firmly.

They sailed on in silence.

"Did you make the chandelier fall tonight?" she asked.

"Enough of your questions!" he roared, so loudly Christine trembled.

"I'd better take you back," he said, more calmly. With a sweep of his cloak, the boat changed direction.

Chapter 7

A disappearing act

The next day, the manager sat in his office with Madame G.

"We must get this phantom! Little Pico is gone. Carlotta's left us. The opera house is falling apart."

"All is not lost. Don't forget we have Christine," said Madame G.

The manager scratched his chin. "You're right. There's something magical about her... Draw up a contract. Carlotta's part is hers!"

That afternoon, posters went up all around Paris advertising the new star of the show.

Before the show, Christine nervously paced her dressing room. It was one thing to do a single performance at the last minute, but quite another to be the leading lady forever.

What if they hate me?

But Christine was a born star. By the end of the show, she felt as if she had played the part all her life.

The show was almost over when the orchestra abruptly stopped playing. The chorus stopped singing and the dancers stopped dancing. The audience shifted uncomfortably in their seats.

Even the temperature seemed to drop. The only person who didn't stop was Christine. She continued to sing. With a crackle, the lights flashed and the stage went dark. Christine let out a scream that sent shivers down everyone's spine.

The lights flared back on, lighting the stage. A trapdoor was open and Christine had vanished.

"Christine!" shouted the Count, from his seat in the front row.

"The phantom must have taken her," he yelled, "through that trapdoor. Follow me!" The manager and Madame G jumped up from their seats and ran after the Count.

Chapter 8

The phantom's lair

The three of them disappeared
under the opera house into the
phantom's secret world. They ran
down the twisting tunnels until
they reached the lake.

"There she is!" The Count pointed to Christine who was in the boat with the phantom. Mist floated around them. "Give her back you beast! I love her!"

"No!" snarled the phantom. "She is mine now. Keep away!"

"It's for the best Count," Christine sobbed.

The phantom turned to Christine.
"I only wanted to be happy, with a
wife and a family."
"But you can!" Christine insisted.
"Who could love me?" he growled.

"Let her go!" shouted the Count. "Don't worry, Christine. I'm coming over!" He began to wade into the lake.

"Get back!" warned the phantom. He flicked his cloak and the water around the boat blazed into flame.

"No!" screamed Christine. "Leave him alone and I'll stay with you."

She reached up and kissed the phantom's cheek where it wasn't hidden by the mask.

Instantly, the fire went out. The phantom fell to his knees, crying.

"No one has ever kissed me. Not even my own mother. You are the kindest person I have ever known."

"I told you, I'm your friend," said Christine. "But you frightened me."

"I'm so sorry," he sobbed, "I was just so lonely..."

Christine put a hand on his shoulder. They could hear police whistles in the distance.

"I must go," the phantom said.

"But..." Christine began and paused in shock.

He had vanished. All that was left in the boat was the phantom's mask. The boat floated to shore.

"Christine!" cried the Count, helping her out. "You're safe now."

They watched as the empty boat floated into the mist.

The manager, Madame G and the police looked around in bewilderment.

Where's he gone?

Christine clutched the mask in her hands. "Goodbye, my angel of music."

Gaston Leroux (1868-1927)

Gaston Leroux was a French writer. He is best known for his novel, *The Phantom of the Opera*. There have been several different film and stage versions of the story. It isn't always clear if the phantom is a ghost or a mad man. The most famous production is Andrew Lloyd Webber's musical which has been performed all over the world.

Series editor: Lesley Sims
Designed by Louise Flutter

First published in 2008 by Usborne Publishing Ltd., Usborne House, 83-85 Saffron Hill, London EC1N 8RT, England. www.usborne.com
Copyright © 2008 Usborne Publishing Ltd.